WOMEN'S PATH TO MANAGEMENT

in the hotel and catering industry

F 331481647 Wom.

First published 1984

ISBN 0 7033 0067 9

Hotel and Catering Industry Training Board
PO Box 18, Ramsey House, Central Square
Wembley, Middlesex HA9 7AP, UK

Printed by Imediaprint Ltd, London

PREFACE

The research study described in this report set out to investigate how women reach management positions in the hotel and catering industry. It is hoped that the results will afford guidance to those concerned with staff development and to women themselves.

The Board commissioned this study as a result of its involvement in a scheme, sponsored by the Manpower Services Commission and administered by the HCITB, whereby grants have been made available for the development of women managers in the hotel and catering industry.

The research was carried out by the HCITB research unit under the direction of Mr T K Reeves, Research Manager. Mrs Caroline Runswick was also closely involved with this study.

The Board would like to acknowledge the assistance of the many individuals who made this study possible.

Marina Aivaliotis
Research Officer
May 1984

CONTENTS

PART 1: OVERVIEW OF THE RESEARCH

1	Introduction	3
2	The aims and methodology	5
3	The status of women in hotels and catering	7
4	Women's career decisions	11
5	Training	13
6	Aspirations	17
7	Attitudes	20
8	Opportunities	21
9	Conclusions and recommendations	22

PART 2: CAREER HISTORIES OF SENIOR MANAGERS

1	Introduction	27
2	Career paths	30
3	Slow progression to senior management	32
4	Calculative career strategies	38
5	Evolutionary career paths	45
6	Examples of mixed strategies	53
7	What are the lessons to be learnt?	59

PART 3: QUESTIONNAIRE

PART 1

OVERVIEW OF THE RESEARCH

1 INTRODUCTION

It is a widely held view that women are disadvantaged in achieving
management positions. This report describes findings from a
research project carried out to discover how far this is true of the
hotel and catering industry, and if so what could be done about it.

The report starts by reviewing women's employment in the hotel and
catering industry, and their opportunities for vocational education
and training that would lead to management. It then summarises the
main findings from interviews carried out with a selection of
managers, both male and female, currently working in the industry.

Women in this study were less likely than men to plan their career.
By contrast to the men, women were content to allow the steps in
their career progression to unfold, taking advantage of
opportunities as they materialised, rather than actively seeking to
create the opportunities they needed. Whilst active career planning
is no guarantee of a successful career, not to plan could place a
person at a disadvantage vis-a-vis those who do.

The research revealed other evidence of women being disadvantaged in
their management career. The traditions of the hotel and catering
industry are against them, in particular the tradition of working up
to management from a craft position, most typically from being a
chef, a job which has always been a male preserve. Contemporary
trends to replace these traditional routes to management by
providing entry to the industry for people with higher diplomas and
degrees in catering still leave women to contend with the obstacles
of an industry that has a legacy of being male dominated.

There were differences, too, in the type of training women received
compared with men, as a result of which their promotions tended to
take them to senior staff positions, for example in personnel,
rather than to the senior operational positions, for example as
general manager or food and beverage manager.

Despite these potential barriers to achievement, the evidence from the women managers in this study shows that, despite its traditions, the industry is one in which it is possible for women to be successful.

The report notes a number of measures that could be taken by the industry and by colleges to facilitate women's path to management. For example, those responsible for management development can ensure that the training received by each sex is balanced. Colleges can offer career guidance to women that goes beyond encouraging them into jobs such as housekeeping that are traditionally associated with women.

But the report also stresses that many of the initiatives need to come from women themselves. To this end, it provides constructive career guidance to women (or men) wishing to make a career in management.

The report includes a selection of career histories showing the step by step progression by which a management position had been achieved. These career histories provide a measure by which the reader can evaluate her or his own career strategy in comparison to others who have succeeded, and provide people who do not think in terms of detailed career planning with alternative models.

This report will be of interest to people with a general interest in women's careers in industry. Its main objective, however, is not academic, but to help the large numbers of women who are currently qualifying on management catering courses to take advantage of the plentiful opportunities that are offered by this industry.

2 THE AIMS AND METHODOLOGY

The principal aim of the research study was to find out how women achieve a successful managerial career in the hotel and catering industry. The second aim was to highlight what obstacles to women's progress exist in the industry, such as discrimination on account of sex, and to suggest how they might be overcome.

Methods of research

The study was conducted by interviewing a small sample of women in the industry selected on the grounds that they had either achieved a managerial position or were aspiring to such a position. Altogether 64 women were interviewed from different sectors of the industry, divided between those who were in senior management positions, those in middle management, and those still looking to be promoted into management. Additionally, a smaller comparable sample of 13 men were interviewed in order to examine their attitudes as selectors, colleagues and competitors of the women interviewed.

Data on the incidence of women in management positions in the hotel and catering industry was drawn from the HCITB's report Manpower in the Hotel and Catering Industry, published in 1978, the follow up research to this study published as Manpower Changes in the Hotel and Catering Industry in 1983, and later research carried out by the HCITB Research Unit for the Education and Training Advisory Council (ETAC) published as Hotel and Catering Skills - Now and in the Future in 1983. Other published sources* were also used.

---

* A bibliography is available on request from the HCITB research unit

Table 1
Women managers as a percentage of all managers in selected
occupational groups in the UK, 1977

Managerial group	% of managers who are women
General management	8.3
Top managers - national government and other non-trading organisations	15.1
General, central, divisional managers - trading organisations	7.9
Managerial (excluding general management)	19.5
Production managers, works managers, works foremen, engineering maintenance managers	3.2
Site and other managers (building and civil engineering)	1.3
Transport managers - air, sea, rail, road, harbour	1.9
Managers - warehousing and materials building	8.8
Office managers	19.8
Managers - wholesale distribution	8.9
Managers - retail distribution	34.9
CATERING AND NON-RESIDENTIAL CLUB MANAGERS	45.4
All managers (including those selected above)	18.8
All managers but excluding those in office, retail and catering and non-residential club management, and publicans	8.5

Source: E C Labour Force Survey 1977 (table taken from MSC report 'No barriers here')

3 THE STATUS OF WOMEN IN HOTELS AND CATERING

A survey carried out in 1977 by the HCITB, Tier I*, indicated that
45 per cent of managers in the hotel and catering industry were
women. On the face of it this seems an impressive statistic,
comparing more than favourably with the incidence of women in the
working population as a whole at that time (41 per cent) and in
other occupational groups such as building and civil engineering
managers (1.3 per cent), transport managers (1.9 per cent), and
office managers (19.8 per cent) - see Table 1 opposite. However,
women represent a very high proportion of the total workforce in the
hotel and catering industry - 73 per cent at the time of the Tier I
survey, and thus one might expect to see more women in management
positions.

Moreover, women managers tend to be concentrated in certain types of
managerial positions and in certain sectors of the industry. The
Tier I data reveals the imbalance. Comparing sectors of the
industry (see Table 2), 59 per cent of managers in industrial
catering, and 70 per cent in other private institutions such as
schools, university halls of residence and nursing homes were women,
while only 29 per cent of managers in restaurants and 38 per cent of
managers in hotels were women.

These figures show clearly that it is in the welfare sectors of the
industry rather than the commercial sectors, that more women achieve
a managerial position.

Data on the proportions of male and female managers holding catering
qualifications, and the types of qualifications they hold is
available from the HCITB's follow-up manpower study, Tier II**.
This found that five per cent of male managers and four per cent
of female managers held a catering degree or other management
qualification.

---

* Tier I published as 'Manpower in the Hotel and Catering Industry',
1978

**Tier II published as 'Manpower Changes in the Hotel and Catering
Industry', 1983

Table 2
Management groups, by sector, by sex and by full and part-time working

Sector	Sex	Senior management		Management	
		Full-time	Part-time	Full-time	Part-time
Hotels	M	20,600	600	20,800	200
	F	15,600	1,300	8,100	1,100
Guesthouses	M	7,000	1,400	–	–
	F	12,600	500	–	–
Restaurants	M	13,500	400	8,900	400
	F	6,900	700	2,000	100
Cafes	M	15,900	900	–	–
	F	15,700	1,900	–	–
Pubs	M	56,000	2,000	4,200	400
	F	44,900	4,500	1,500	500
Clubs	M	11,000	1,500	2,100	100
	F	5,000	2,000	800	400
Industrial catering	M	4,900	100	–	–
	F	6,800	400	–	–
Other private institutions*	M	1,200	100	–	–
	F	2,500	500	–	–
Total**		258,900		51,600	

*Nursing homes, university halls of residence etc
**Figures for Local Authorities and DHSS not included
Source: HCITB, 'Manpower in the Hotel and Catering Industry', 1978

Table 3
Highest level qualification held, by skill level, by sex

| Qualification | MANAGEMENT | | | | SUPERVISORY | | | |
| | Male | | Female | | Male | | Female | |
	Nos	%	Nos	%	Nos	%	Nos	%
Hotel & catering:								
Degree or management level	50	5	24	4	6	1	17	2
OND	9	1	12	2	21	4	5	0.7
NEBSS	1	0.1	3	0.5	–	–	5	0.7
Craft level	116	12	48	8	111	21	110	14
Any degree or HND	5	0.5	4	0.6	5	0.9	4	0.5
Base of percentages	976		617		529		801	

Source: HCITB, Tier II survey

Table 4
Proportion of students on hotel and catering management level courses, by sex

	Degree %	OND/Diploma %	HND/Higher Diploma %	HCIMA %
Male	32	30	30	47
Female	68	70	70	53
Base of percentages	237	1,431	648	536

Source: ETAC, 'Hotel and Catering Skills – Now and in the Future', 1983

More male managers held catering craft qualifications than female managers (Table 3). 12 per cent of male managers held a City and Guilds craft level catering qualification as their highest qualification compared to eight per cent of female managers in the industry.

A comparison of the numbers of men and women pursuing different kinds of hotel and catering courses in colleges, including those at management level is available from data collected in the research carried out by the HCITB for ETAC*. From Table 4, which indicates the proportions of male and female students on management level courses it is found that 68 per cent of the students on degree courses were female and only 32 per cent male. On OND/diploma courses 70 per cent were female, and 30 per cent male. These ratios do not reflect the numbers holding managerial positions in the industry.

Barriers to women's advancement

This evidence shows that women do reach managerial positions in the hotel and catering industry, but more opportunities occur in the welfare than the commercial sectors, and the ratio of female to male managers does not in general, reflect the numbers studying for management qualifications.

This suggests that barriers to women's advancement in the industry do exist. In the following sections data obtained from the interviews with the sample of aspiring and successful women, and their comparable male colleagues is reported on.

---

* Published as 'Hotel and Catering Skills - Now and in the Future', by the HCITB on behalf of the Education and Training Advisory Council, 1983

4 WOMEN'S CAREER DECISIONS

Women's career decisions were found to be influenced closely by
personal and family considerations. Respondents stressed the
conflicts between career and family commitments. Few of the women
in the sample, who had reached a senior management position, had
children, many were not married. The women interviewed expressed
strong feelings on their need to make sacrifices. They seemed aware
that the hours of work in many sectors of the hotel and catering
industry were incompatible with domestic obligations.

By contrast, all six of the male senior managers interviewed were
family men, and while this is too small a number for a statistically
valid comparison, few would wish to dispute that these domestic
circumstances are typical of many male managers.

Despite their awareness of these conflicts between career and family
commitments, the women who had reached senior management positions
gave no indication that they had been hampered by them.

As observed in the previous section, more men than women in
managerial positions held a craft qualification. This reflects
the fact that for men a typical route to management is to work up
from a craft job. The greater proportion of women than men on
management level courses suggests that women are relying more on
attaining their position through acquiring an appropriate level of
qualification for it, and that if they only had a craft
qualification there is less chance of their abilities being
recognised and/or developed as is the case with men.

A consequence of women generally following a more formal route to
management than men is that women managers tend to have held
comparatively few positions during their career.

Also, as evidence from other research* and indeed the findings of
the present study show, women who are receiving promotion are doing
so at an earlier age than their male counterparts.

The men interviewed had clearly planned their careers with consider-
able foresight, with defined goals and time scales. Again, while
there may have been an element of exaggeration in the extent of their
foresight, the notion of planning a career is typical of male
managers. By contrast among the women interviewed, there was a
distinct absence of career planning. Women who were in senior
management positions, when asked to reflect on their route to
promotion, were generally unable to identify any conscious strategy
that they had been following other than identifying a wide and
varied experience as being a good strategy to adopt; while those who
were still aspiring to a management position had no time scale for
achieving their goals, or even had any clear idea of where they
wanted to be in a few years' time, other than a general aspiration
to have moved upwards.

---

* Derived from Tier II data (published as 'Manpower Changes in the
  Hotel and Catering Industry') 1983 in conjunction with the Institute
  of Manpower Studies

5 TRAINING

The study investigated what in company training and company
sponsored training members of the sample had received during their
career. Striking differences emerged between the men and the women,
and whilst the comparison is based on small numbers, the
nature of these differences was so distinctive that they do appear
to reflect the differing career paths of the two groups.

First, a small number of the women managers in the sample had
received no company sponsored training at all during their career.
This cannot be attributed to the mischance of working for an
employer who did not offer in-company training, for - at least as
far as their present employer was concerned - this was not the
case.

Second, where women had received company sponsored training, the
type of course they had gone on was typically very different to the
type of course their male counterparts had taken. The findings,
presented in Table 5 show the numbers of males and females who had
received certain types of training. (It should be noted that
overlap does occur in the numbers since most respondents had been on
more than one course.)

The men's training had almost exclusively been concerned with
developing their managerial skills in the widest sense, covering
areas like principles and practice of management, and financial
management. By contrast, the women managers had taken courses
concerned with the ancillary management functions, particularly
personnel management. Courses attended included selection
interviewing, appraisals, training, sales and marketing, courses
preparing them for a staff role rather than an operational or line
management role. Yet the high proportion of women on hotel and
catering courses suggests that they are in fact seeking a career in
operational management.

Table 5
Numbers of male and female respondents in the study who had received training

Type of training	Male		Female	
	Nos	%	Nos	%
NONE	–	–	6	10
Craft, health & safety, other	5	38	48	83
Sales & marketing	2	15	10	17
Industrial relations	3	23	11	20
Personal skills	1	8	2	3
Decision making/ problem solving	3	23	1	2
Appraisal	1	8	6	10
Interviewing/selection	1	8	16	28
Management principles	6	46	17	26
Training officer	1	8	–	–
Management of inter- personal relations	1	8	4	7
Accountancy/purchasing	2	15	9	16
Base of percentages		13		58

It was however not altogether clear from the interviews whether women managers had pursued this kind of training because they were going into, or were already in, an ancillary function, or whether they ended up in these positions because of the type of training they had taken.

What was clear was that they were not conscious of receiving a different type of managerial training to men.

A further difference in the type of training received by men and women in the sample was that a far higher percentage of women had been sent on a number of courses normally linked with craft training, for example, health and safety, fire prevention and first aid. It is possible that this reflects their different career paths, and men would have undertaken these types of courses while working in craft positions, before promotion to management.

Whatever the rationale for women receiving different types of training to men, the outcome was that they tended to have become specialised in a particular managerial function, and their scope for transferring from one area to another was limited.

Table 6

Reasons given for choosing a career in catering by respondents on management level courses in the ETAC research sample

Reason	Male		Female		Total	
	Nos	%	Nos	%	Nos	%
Enjoyed cooking at school	3	4	11	12	14	9
Like cooking	15	22	21	23	36	23
Meeting people	18	26	24	26	42	26
Good career	17	25	14	15	31	19
Previous work experience	16	24	18	20	34	21
Variety	10	15	14	15	24	15
Ambition and interest	9	13	25	27	34	21
Stimulating work	10	15	8	9	18	11
Course content	7	10	7	8	4	3
Second choice	4	6	8	9	12	8
Family interest	12	18	14	15	26	16
Creative craft	3	4	6	7	9	6
Mobility	8	12	7	8	15	9
Like service	2	3	2	2	4	3
Know people who did catering	–	–	1	1	1	1
Other	23	34	29	32	52	33
Base of percentages	68		91		159	

16

6 ASPIRATIONS

The evidence reported in the previous sections has suggested that there may be some influences outside women's control which direct them to certain types of managerial position or limit their attainment. It also needs to be considered how far their career in management is influenced by their own aspirations and attitudes. Although the women interviewed were, and in most cases always had been, ambitious for themselves, they had not defined career aspirations appropriate for achieving these ambitions.

This lack of match between general ambition and defined aspiration is reflected in data obtained from the research on student career aspirations conducted for the ETAC project on the education and training needs of the industry.

Male and female students interviewed on management level courses shared some reasons for wanting a career in catering, enjoyment of cooking and the kind of life it offered for example, however, other motives were very different (Table 6 opposite). More of the female students interviewed were going into catering through interest and realisation of a long-term ambition, whereas more male than female students thought of catering as a good career with good employment potential and scope for promotion. This may have an important bearing on how women plan their future careers.

Although the male and female students shared similar aspirations about the kind of job they hoped to have five years after leaving college or university (Table 7), the type of job they expected to obtain immediately on leaving differed (Table 8). The women seemed to expect their immediate jobs on leaving college to be at a lower level than did the men, regardless of course followed. This is well exemplified by the fact that only 38 per cent of the women compared with 55 per cent of the men expected to get a position as a management trainee immediately on leaving college.

17

Table 7
Type of job hoped for in five years' time by respondents on management
level courses in the ETAC research sample

Job	Male		Female	
	Nos	%	Nos	%
Hotel manager	9	16	13	16
Management trainee	2	4	3	4
Assistant manager	13	23	18	22
Accounts	2	4	1	1
Personnel staff	1	2	2	2
Front office manager	2	4	–	–
Receptionist	–	–	1	1
Catering manager	6	11	11	14
Head chef	1	2	2	2
Sous chef	1	2	–	–
Chef	–	–	1	1
Domestic bursar	–	–	3	4
Restaurant manager	–	–	1	1
Head waiter silver service	–	–	1	1
Waiter silver service	1	2	–	–
Sales/marketing	1	2	1	1
General manager	15	27	19	23
Deputy manager	1	2	1	1
Proprietor	1	2	2	2
Forces catering	–	–	1	1
Base of percentages	56		81	

Table 8
Type of job hoped for immediately after leaving college by respondents
on management level courses in the ETAC research sample

Job	Male		Female	
	Nos	%	Nos	%
Hotel manager	–	–	1	1
Management trainee	32	55	31	38
Assistant manager	12	21	19	23
Accounts	1	2	–	–
Clerical staff	–	–	1	1
Front office manager	–	–	1	1
Receptionist	1	2	1	1
Catering manager	–	–	4	5
Chef	–	–	3	4
Kitchen supervisor	–	–	4	5
Chef specialist	–	–	1	1
Commis chef	4	7	2	2
Domestic bursar	–	–	3	4
House manager	–	–	2	2
Restaurant manager	1	2	1	1
Waiter silver service	2	3	1	1
Waiter plate service	1	2	–	–
General manager	4	7	1	1
Number of respondents	58		81	

The findings of the present study substantiate this result. Women interviewed had generally started with lower level jobs than their qualifications warranted, although they tended not to be aware of this having happened to them. There was a widespread view amongst these respondents that it was important that they acquired adequate knowledge before attempting to move upwards. This did not seem to be a view held by the men interviewed, and could be interpreted as reflecting a lack of confidence on the part of the women.

Whether this is the reason or whether women display a more considered approach to each career move, their low level aspirations at the outset of their career are likely to have long term repercussions on their subsequent advancement compared with men.

7 ATTITUDES

In considering how women's careers are advanced or held back an important factor is their own attitude towards the role of women in management. In order to explore this, a set of attitude scales developed specially to measure attitudes towards women as managers* was administered to the present sample.

A surprising finding was that many of the women seemed to share the stereotyped views that men often hold. For example, it was believed that women lacked the confidence to push themselves; that they are not ambitious enough; that they are influenced by their emotions and this affects their managerial behaviour; that they are undesirable as employees because of pregnancy and problems connected with menstruation; that they are not competitive enough and that they are not aggressive enough.

Not all the women interviewed subscribed to all these negative images of women as managers, but all of them gave a negative response on at least one out of the 21 attitude items they were asked about.

It is difficult to interpret these findings. The women respondents were asked to reply for women in general, and not for themselves in particular. While some may have been projecting their own views about themselves, it is more likely that most were generalising about women other than themselves.

While it may be the case that the respondents were excepting themselves from these stereotyped views, it might be regarded as unfortunate that a group of women who have succeeded in their careers should share opinions which are commonly held to obstruct women's advancement.

---

* The scale was developed by Lawrence H Peters, James R Terborg and Janet Taynor, as a specific measure of attitudes towards women as managers.

8 OPPORTUNITIES

The evidence from other research (see Section 2) does suggest that the hotel and catering industry offers career opportunities for women in management. The women interviewed in this study recognised this. Indeed there was a consensus of opinion that it was 'a good industry for women'. The opportunities were there if women were willing to push themselves.

On the other hand, opportunities for women in the industry are undoubtedly restricted and those that do exist are largely confined to particular sectors of the industry and to certain 'acceptable' jobs. Some sectors, notably pubs and clubs, were considered especially bad in terms of opportunities for women. Industrial catering (both direct and contract) and hospitals were considered good sectors not only for the career opportunities, but also for the convenience of hours and conditions of work.

The existence of what are regarded as 'acceptable' jobs for women results in them specialising more than men. Thus women managers tend to be found primarily in the personnel, sales, training and marketing functions rather than in the operational or line side of catering.

Data revealed in the research studies described in Section 2, confirms that these perceptions are a true representation of the state of the industry.

9   CONCLUSIONS AND RECOMMENDATIONS

One of the principal aims of this study was to highlight
constructive courses of action for overcoming barriers to women's
progress as managers in the industry. The findings of this report
confirm that barriers do exist especially for those trying to make
inroads into areas of work less associated with women. They suggest
that there is still a great deal to be done in overcoming them.

There are three main bodies or groups of people in a position to
take action.

Managers responsible for the personnel and training function

This study indicates that women have received different training
from men, usually restricted to specific areas of work, ie personnel
and training, while men have received much broader management
training. Women are thus being disadvantaged, with reduced scope
for movement within the industry or to other areas.

Managers responsible for the training and development of staff are
in a position to correct this imbalance, by ensuring that women
receive the same training opportunities as their male counterparts.
In due course the competition for management positions would become
a more equitable one. As a high proportion of those responsible for
the development of staff are in fact women (it has been noted that
women tend to specialise in ancillary or staff roles) this
transition should be easier to achieve.

Thus, more varied and broader training should be available to women,
and where it is already available to them, they should be encouraged
to take it.

Secondly, this study has highlighted how at the beginning of many
women's careers, no definite strategy or career path has been
considered. It is important that the danger is avoided of following
a route already established by other women, into an 'acceptable'
area of work, without being aware that this is happening, or that
alternatives do exist.

Thus women need more constructive guidance on the options available
to them. Furthermore, at reviews and appraisals, other
possibilities for wider development and cross training should be
closely examined, so that women could have greater scope to move
into any area of work they choose.

Colleges

On hotel and catering courses at management level, the proportion
of female students is much higher than male. Indeed the evidence in
this study suggests that women tend to seek a career in management
based on management qualifications and do not achieve that position
through a craft route. Thus colleges can play a large part in
influencing career decisions made by women, and can play a far more
active part in the long-term development of their female students.

It is vital therefore that there should be adequate career guidance
during college courses with more definite information given to the
students on the options open to them. Those areas which have
traditionally been difficult for women to get into should be
explored more by students from the time they are at college, and not
necessarily accepted as closed options.

Colleges can play an important role through creating the right
student environment, in helping break down misconceptions about
certain jobs being more suitable for one sex than another.

Aspiring women in the industry

The most positive action must come from the women themselves.

If women wish to make a career in hotel and catering management and
wish to compete on an equal level with their male colleagues, the
first step they must take is to carefully define their career plan.
Some of the successful women interviewed in this study did not in
fact do so, but this does not lessen the value of defining a career
plan. The example of their male colleagues who did so suggests it
may be a more assured method of reaching high management status than
relying solely on ability and conscientious work.

The second step is that women must not be passive about their
personal development and training. They must ensure that they do
get training opportunities and in a wide range of management
activities, as relevant as possible to their long-term plans.

Thirdly, they should seek a wide variety of experience. This seems
to have been a valuable asset for the 'successful' women
interviewed, whether they took a company route or an industry route.
A range of experience gives greater flexibility of movement within
the industry generally.

Fourthly, a career in this industry can be combined with family
commitments if this is desired. As the findings of this study and
others show, when women progress in the industry, they tend to do so
quickly and at an early age. Women can therefore achieve a senior
status before giving up work to have a family, and later re-enter
the industry at a reasonably high management level.

PART 2

CAREER HISTORIES OF
SENIOR MANAGERS

1 INTRODUCTION

In this part of the report career histories are presented of 12 of the women and men interviewed for the study. They are intended to provide practical illustration of how people, especially women, have succeeded in reaching senior positions in the hotel and catering industry.

It is not possible to draw out from these career histories any golden rules by which people may gain more rapid promotion, but they do illustrate the diverse routes through which people have got on in the industry.

Many reached their position in senior or a high middle management by their late twenties or early thirties, and might be termed 'high fliers'.

Discrepancies may be apparent in the classification used for senior and middle management as a result of differences in job title between sectors and companies. The classification system used for senior and middle management was based on that developed for the HCITB and ETAC studies, mentioned in Part 1, and also took into consideration the respondent's own account of his/her level of responsibility, number of subordinate staff, reporting relationships, function etc.

Some 'high flyers' have succeeded by staying with one company since entering the industry. Others have progressed by moving from one company to another using the industry as a whole as a career ladder. Some have obtained managerial level qualifications in catering before entering the industry. Others have succeeded without the support of qualifications, or have obtained them later on in their career. Some have been successful by specialising in their career, for example in line management or in one of the ancillary functions such as personnel. Others have had a diversity of experience and been just as successful.

It may be tempting to make certain generalisations about the routes high flying women, and men, follow on their way up. These career histories illustrate that individuals are not constrained by generalisations. There is no right, nor wrong, superior or inferior way of getting to the top. It is possible to succeed by following virtually any route.

In Part 1 it was noted that most women managers in the study lacked a clear career strategy while the men tended to plan their careers. They thought in terms of career models, planned how far they should have progressed by a certain age, decided what they needed to do to develop their abilities and ensured they obtained the right training and job experiences. Above all they had clear promotion goals.

Since there are clearly more men than women in senior managerial positions, it might be tempting to advise women with ambition to take a leaf out of the men's book and adopt a similarly 'calculative' career strategy. But, a number of women, and men, in the study have been successful without doing this. A substantial proportion of those who had reached senior management or high middle management positions at a young age, had done so without carefully calculating each step in their progress. This group of people had been content to let events take their course, seizing opportunities when they presented themselves, but essentially following an 'evolutionary' career path, allowing their career to unfold or evolve naturally.

The career histories

Of the 77 people interviewed for the study, 25 were in senior management positions. Career histories of nine of these are presented in this report, carefully selected to give the reader an adequate range of examples on which to base conclusions. A further three career histories of people in middle management positions, and whose careers were still developing, are also presented. Further career histories are available on request from the HCITB research unit.

28

Each career history is presented in a standard format and gives details of the person's qualifications, career progression and key factors that motivated and influenced them.

One of the biggest problems facing women is the lack of models and precedents to follow. It is hoped that the career histories included in this part of the report and the conclusions drawn from them will show an emerging pattern with which the reader can identify.

2 CAREER PATHS

A review of the nine career histories of managers who had reached
senior positions indicates that they can generally be classified
according to whether or not the person had carefully planned his or
her career.

The CALCULATIVE or EVOLUTIONARY approach to a career are two very
distinct strategies used to reach a senior management position,
irrespective of the actual path taken. Of course the steps taken,
and the actual career decisions made are important, but more
significant is the planning and intent behind them.

The respondents following a 'calculative' career path believed in
career planning, had a career model in their mind, and largely
explained their progression by reference to their model, even though
their plans may have been disrupted in practice. An element of
retrospective rationalising may have existed, however, and their
career may not have followed quite such a logical progression as
that reported at the time of the interview, but this does not
detract from the nature of the strategy.

By contrast, those following an 'evolutionary' career path, were
similarly successful, but their explanations for their success made
no reference to any clear or conscious strategy for getting on.
Indeed some went out of their way to stress that they were not
'career minded' or were not prepared to engage in the 'politicking'
that they believed others used to get on. This strategy of waiting
for one's career to evolve is, nevertheless, a strategy if only by
default.

The careers of the high fliers seem to have two characteristics in
common, regardless of whether the career strategy was 'calculative'
or 'evolutionary'.

One was that the ambition to acquire high level management status existed whether or not there was a definite plan. This was critical. The decision made at any turning point in the careers of the high fliers was always governed by the rewards it would yield long and/or short-term.

The second characteristic was the existence of some kind of threshold or take-off point, when people seem to change gear and start moving firmly upwards. For those who had reached a senior position by their late twenties or early thirties, this take-off point came in the person's early twenties. After an initial period of gaining experience, without being too selective about the jobs done, the high flier seemed then to get a job with a definite aim.

From this take-off point, given that the individual succeeds, begins the ascent to more and more senior management positions.

This first key opportunity is a critical stage as far as career progression is concerned. (This turning point is illustrated in the career histories that follow, by a dotted line in the job history chart, showing at what age this particular career move was made.)

Many of those interviewed for this study talked about 'luck' and 'being in the right place at the right time'. Indeed there may have been an element of luck in their careers, but the emergence of a career turning point is such a common feature that not too much weight should be attached to the 'luck' explanations, particularly in the case of those who had actively planned their career.

Discussion of these two characteristics of 'high flyers' would be incomplete without recording the value of obtaining the backing and support of immediate superiors early on in a career, and secondly of the value of making one's mark and being remembered for it.

3 SLOW PROGRESSION TO SENIOR MANAGEMENT

The first two career histories (pages 34 and 36) provide an
historical backdrop. They would serve as cautionary tales about
the penalties of leaving one's career to develop by chance, except
that opportunities today are so much greater for the aspiring
manager that the risks are probably not the same.

The career histories selected are of a man and a woman, both aged
55 at the time of the study, who had embarked on their hotel and
catering career just after the second world war. This was a time
when there were virtually no opportunities to gain a managerial
level qualification in hotels and catering and for most people the
only way to get on was through experience.

The man (career history 1) started as office boy in a brewery at
the age of 14 with no educational qualifications and slowly but
surely worked his way up, first reaching a management position in
his mid-twenties, to become area sales manager for another brewery
by the age of 50. He was still in this position at the time of the
study, and he believed, at the age of 55, he was unlikely to
progress further. His original entry into the industry was
fortuitous: brewery office boy was the first job he found near to
home. While not unambitious he had been content to let his career
evolve with little positive initiative on his part, certainly none
that he could recall.

The woman (career history 2) had left school at 17 with a higher
certificate. Like the man, she too had started her career at the
bottom of the industry just after the war. She had also entered
the industry fortuitously, encouraged to do so by her father who
felt that hotels and catering might offer prospects for someone
with no qualifications. But unlike her office boy counterpart, she
had set about gaining more systematically a variety of experiences,
as a chef, waitress and receptionist, which would help her
progress.

32

On the other hand, apart from a determination that she would not stay running a canteen all her life, she had no clear idea of what her next steps upward would be. She thus had no plan of action for pursuing her career.

At the time of the reseach, at the age of 55, she had just been promoted to director of operations for a contract catering firm and had a seat on the board. However, she felt that she had probably now reached a plateau in her career.

Both persons' careers were interrupted by forces outside their control, national service in the case of the man, having to leave work for about a year to nurse a sick mother in the case of the woman.

Although it took them a long time to work their way up, the circumstances and opportunities for development in today's industry would usually allow for speedier advancement.

CAREER HISTORY 1

Job and personal details

Job title: Area sales manager
Level: Senior management
Type of establishment: Large brewery company

Sex: Male
Age: 55 years
Marital status: Married
Qualifications: None
Training: Various HCITB training courses
Years in industry: 42 (including a 3 year break
                   whilst in the army)

Job history

AGE	CAREER MOVES	
14 years	General office boy - brewery	
15 years	Office clerk to the brewery director	
18 years	National service	
21 years	Managed house department in a junior position and worked his way up to manager of the department	
----------	--	
27 years	Sales manager	) with
32 years	Training manager	) present
37 years	Area manager - catering	) company, a
45 years	Area manager - pubs	) brewery
50 years	Present job	)

Career outline

The respondent left school at 14 years of age and became a general office boy at a brewery company. After this he became an office clerk to the director of a brewery company. National service intervened and the respondent was away from his job for three years.

On completion of national service he returned to his previous company and joined the newly created managed house department in a junior position. He spent six years in this department obtaining promotion and learning most of the different department activities, finally reaching the position of manager. It was an important time for him, a time of great career development. But as it was over 30 years ago, he could not recall the precise duration of each stage.

He then joined his present company 28 years ago and had since worked through a number of different activities within the company.

The influences affecting choice of catering as a career

The respondent's reason for going into catering was that it was the first job that he could find in the area in which he lived. He knew that there would be opportunities for career advancement, although he felt that he might just as easily have gone into the textile or hosiery industry.

Further career aspirations

Although the respondent enjoyed what he was doing, he was not really looking to progress any further with his career.

He aspired to reaching a directorship, but did not feel that he had much chance of this due to his age.

CAREER HISTORY 2

Job and personal details

Job title: Group director of operations/board
                              director
Level: Senior management
Type of establishment: Independent contract catering firm

Sex: Female
Age: 55 years
Marital status: Married
Qualifications: Scottish Higher Level Certificate
                              Matron and housewifery course -
                              Royal College of Domestic Science (1949)
Training: MHCIMA (late 1970's)
Years in industry: 34

Job history

AGE	CAREER MOVES
17 years	Voluntary Aid Detachment - Royal Navy
20 years	College (see above)
21 years	Domestic supervisor - Royal Infirmary
22-26 years	Waitress) Working abroad in
	Commis chef) various establish-
	General assistant) ments learning as
	much as possible
	about craft skills
	in the hotel and
	catering industry
----------	--
26 years	Returned home to nurse sick mother
27 years	Manageress in a biscuit making factory
35 years	Left due to pregnancy
36 years	Returned as an assistant area supervisor - industrial catering company
38-48 years	Joined present company to assist in its formation and for 10 years managed various units as they opened
48 years	Group manager - promoted to this newly created position
52 years	Group manager/board director - two activities carried out simultaneously
55 years	Present job

Career outline

This respondent's career seemed to 'take off' at the age of 27 when
she worked for eight years as a manager in a biscuit making
factory. She considered this to be part of her catering career and
describes it as giving her "good business training".

After a short break in her career (see above) her present boss managing director/chairman) heard about her through a mutual friend and asked her to help him for a short time by assisting the area supervisor in another company. This was the first time she had been involved with industrial catering.

This same man then went into partnership with a colleague and decided to set up the present company, taking the respondent with him. He offered her the position of unit manager on the understanding that as the company grew so would her job.

"And from then on it just all happened. I think it just evolved. I didn't set out with any great ambition to become a director, it wasn't even on my mind. I just knew I wouldn't remain running a canteen forever because I need new challenge and stimulation.

"If I had had children it would have changed the course of my subsequent career. I wouldn't have stayed at home with them, but things wouldn't have happened as they did."

The influences affecting choice of catering as a career

The respondent had wanted to be a nurse, hence her attachment to the VAD after the war. Her father encouraged her to go into catering because she had no qualifications.

Further career aspirations

The respondent said she would always avoid any position that could be described as a 'desk job', that is a corporate level job. She was 'first and foremost a caterer'.

Her current job (which she had acquired only the day before the interview took place) involved extending the company's sphere of operations. She felt however, that once she had established her new role she would have to take more of a back seat to allow others to progress and that her job would then become an advisory one, without her making further substantial progress in her career.

4 CALCULATIVE CAREER STRATEGIES

Calculative career strategies are by no means confined to men: career history 3 is of a woman who obtained a catering qualification at management level and reached the position of general manager of a hotel by the age of 30. Career history 4 is of a man with a similar level qualification who had also became a hotel general manager at the age of 30. Each had pursued a calculative strategy for achieving their position.

What were the kinds of tactics that these two people used to plan their advancement? Were there any special circumstances that they were able to take advantage of?

In both cases an early take-off point was probably critical. The man having worked abroad for 18 months to gain experience, obtained a job as chief steward at the age of 21. This gave him his first supervisory role and from this stage, he progressed rapidly.

Support from their superiors was critical in capitalising on the take-off point and, in contrast to many of those pursuing an evolutionary path to senior management, these respondents did not treat this support in a passive way. They were actively concerned to ensure that they were included in any current management development plan.

In fact the woman manager described in career history 3 created her own management development programme. When, as a trainee for reception and accounts, she found that there was no structured training programme, she succeeded in having a two year training course specially tailored to her needs as she perceived them. She explained her tactics for getting on: "Each move has been consciously slightly sideways and upwards - on the way learning about different sides of the hotel industry."

She tried working in personnel for a while to see what it involved, but never lost sight of the fact that the purpose of this period in an ancillary function was to broaden her experience. She did not

allow herself to be side-tracked. Looking to the future, she
wanted to have her own business: "If I can work for someone else
for a salary, I may as well do it for myself and get it all."

This purposefulness that marks out people pursuing a calculative
career strategy is well illustrated by the man. He set himself
career targets linked to age: "I tend to map out my career in five
year modules. At 21 I had decided that I would be a general
manager by 31 years. I didn't do too badly - I made it at 33."

Pursuing a calculative career strategy is not, however, always
accompanied by consistent single-mindedness in following out one's
intentions.

Looking back, the man reflected: "I deviated from a line to a
staff role (purchasing manager) - maybe I should have moved out of
the staff role sooner than I did." But looking ahead, he was still
thinking in terms of time-linked targets: "In the next five to six
years, I see myself consolidating the general management position
and I will be looking to take up a corporate role."

In characterising approaches to careers as 'calculative', it does
not necessarily follow that the person made a calculated choice to
make their career in the hotel and catering industry. There were
often fortuitous or chance reasons why people entered the industry
in the first place. The distinguishing feature is that, once in
the industry, they formed a clear vision of what they needed to do
to get on, and took active steps to realise their ambitions.

This translation of ambitions into a concrete career plan is as
much an attitude of mind as a tactic. It relies on having a clear
career goal in the first place.

CAREER HISTORY 3

Job and personal details

Job title: General manager
Level: Senior management
Type of establishment: Large city hotel

Sex: Female
Age: 32 years
Marital status: Single
Qualifications: 8 'O'levels
                              2 year Basic Catering Diploma (1969)
                              1 year MHCIMA
Training: Two year training course specially
                              tailored to meet her needs when
                              first a trainee (1969)
                              Cranfield Management Course (1981)
                              Short courses in: supervision, appraisal
                              selection, communications
Years in industry: 16

Job history

AGE	CAREER MOVES	
16 years	College	
19 years	Trainee (accounts/reception)	)
19 years	Decimalisation trainer	)
--------	------------------------------------	)---------
20 years	Junior assistant manager	)
20½ years	Food and beverage manager	) large
22 years	Banqueting manager	) hotel
23½ years	House manager	) group
25 years	Personnel manager	)
26½ years	Deputy general manager	)
30 years	General manager - present job	)

Career outline

After leaving college 13 years ago the respondent joined the
company as a trainee with a view to becoming involved in accounts
and reception. But within nine months she had requested a transfer
to something new and became involved in decimalisation training.
      She felt that she had her first big break into junior
management when she decided that she did not only want to do
reception. At this time she "just happened to fall into the hands
of a general manager who was very pro-female". He felt that women
managers had a great deal to offer the catering industry.
      By her account she was given some challenging jobs to do and
did them well and was noticed for it; also being the only woman at
the time was an advantage.

40

At this time there were no structured training programmes, but she was able to dictate her needs and requirements and training was specially provided for her.

She was encouraged by friends and family to ask and push for what she wanted and she said that "each move has been consciously slightly sideways and upwards - on the way learning about different sides of the hotel industry". Thus she tried other disciplines and deviated from her path, but always had in mind her intention of becoming a general caterer and not a specialist.

"At a college careers talk I liked the sound of what was on offer from the two big companies which had sent representatives, and I resolved to join the one that I eventually worked for."

The influences affecting choice of catering as a career

"I went to a competitive school where the girls were very clever. When I compared myself to them I didn't think I was as bright as they were. I didn't want to be a secretary but I didn't know what to do. I got all the local college prospectuses and eliminated what I didn't want. The catering courses sounded very varied so I did that. I stayed in catering not because of the catering side but because I liked the administrative side".

Further career aspirations

The respondent's situation had changed eight months before the the interview when the hotel was sold by the hotel company with which she had been since the start of her career.

Had this change not taken place, the respondent would have remained in her present position for two to three years, moved as a general manager to a larger hotel and within ten years she would have gone to a corporate level job. But the change forced her to think about her next step earlier than anticipated. She had now turned her thoughts to starting up her own business, a small hotel of her own perhaps or seeking financial backing or a partnership to purchase something larger.

"The last six months have proved to me how much I know, and if I can work for someone else for a salary I may as well do it for myself and get it all".

CAREER HISTORY 4

Job and personal details

Job title: General manager
Level: Senior management
Type of establishment: Large airport hotel - one of a group

Sex: Male
Age: 34 years
Marital status: Married
Qualifications: 7 'O'levels
                         3 years management course leading to
                         MHCIMA (1969)
                         National Trade Development
                         Association Diploma (1969)
                         Membership of Institute of Purchasing and
                         Supply (1971)
Training: General management courses
                         Management development programme
                         (2 year period)
                         Decision making course
                         Sales and marketing
                         Management grid courses - Coverdale
                         Institute (5 x 2 weeks modules)
Years in industry: 18

Job history

AGE	CAREER MOVES
16½ years	Left school and worked in a hotel and with parents in family restaurant
17 years	3 year final membership course of HCIMA
20 years	Commis chef - London hotel
	Commis chef) Worked abroad to
	Waiter) consolidate learning
20½ years	Chief steward
22 years	Food and beverage controller)hotels
23 years	Purchasing manager)within a
26 years	Materials manager)parent
28 years	Food and beverage manager)company -
30 years	Executive assistant manager)major
31 years	Executive food and beverage)interests
	manager)not hotels
33 years	General manager - present job

Career outline

Until he was old enough to take his HCIMA course the respondent
spent time working in a hotel and with his family in their
restaurant.

After qualifying, he travelled abroad gaining experience in various European countries, before returning to England to his first job in a supervisory role as chief steward. His next move, to food and beverage controller, seems to have been the most decisive of his career.

The move out of operations and into purchasing was because he wanted exposure as a member of the management team. He felt he was too young to achieve this in line management and this quick promotion could be followed by a period of consolidation, where age, experience and salary would catch up with each other. He also got at this time the chance to work with people who had a great deal more experience than himself.

He took exams in purchasing and remained in this more specialist area before returning to main line operations a move he found difficult because... "one tends to get branded in one particular role."

The respondent described his career plan as structured: "I tend to map out my career in five year modules. At 21 I had decided that I would be a general manager by 31, although at that time I saw a line management approach to it - purchasing did not figure in my plans at all. I deviated from a line to a staff role - maybe I should have moved out of the staff role sooner than I did."

The influences affecting choice of catering as a career

The respondent attributed his interest in catering to the fact that he lived in a catering environment for most of his young life. His parents owned a restaurant above which they lived and he felt that the ties with catering were very strong.

Initially he enjoyed the technical side of catering rather than the service aspect of it. He had since acquired a liking for customer contact and the pressurised nature of catering. Whilst at college the respondent recognised that hotel and catering was a growth industry, and that there would be scope for career development.

Further career aspirations

The respondent saw himself consolidating his present position in general management within the next five years. He would expect to have two or three more general management positions to take him into his 40's. "I will then be looking to take up a corporate role, for example director of operations within a large company. The urge to own my own business has not bitten me yet, but it may catch up with me - certainly not until my late 40's, early 50's."

5 EVOLUTIONARY CAREER PATHS

Three career histories have been selected to illustrate
evolutionary career paths. Career history 5 is of a woman who
started as a hotel and catering operative and became a personnel
and training manager by the age of 34. She had made a positive
decision to enter the hotel and catering industry but her career
within it was unplanned. Career history 6 is of a woman who
entered the industry with a craft qualification and became general
catering manager for a contract catering firm by the age of 35.
Career history 7 is of a woman with a qualification in fashion
design who entered the hotel and catering industry in her early
30's after a variety of sales jobs and quickly became director of
sales and marketing for a large city hotel.

What these people had in common was that they had allowed their
career to unfold, seizing opportunities as they occurred but not
deliberately setting out to create these opportunites for
themselves. In some cases the ambition to reach high management
status was secondary to making a career in catering, and indeed the
choice of catering for a career may also have been fortuitous: "My
parents felt that some sort of further education would be a stop-
gap ... there being very few options open where I lived - so I
simply fell into catering." (Career history 6.)

The respondent in career history 7 also entered the industry by
chance, her experience in sales and involvement in the tourism
industry, notably car hire and travel, enabled her to cross over
into catering. However she regarded herself as a business woman
first and a caterer second.

These three examples illustrate the level of success that can be
reached following evolutionary career paths. Further career plans
were apparent in the cases of career histories 5 and 6.

CAREER HISTORY 5

Job and personal details

Job title: Executive personnel and training
                                    manager
Level: Senior management
Type of establishment: Outside catering operations

Sex: Female
Age: 37 years
Marital status: Single
Qualifications: 7 'O' levels
                                    Diploma in Management Studies (1980)
Training: Management development course
                                    Interviewing skills
                                    Selling course
                                    Diploma RIPHH
                                    Cranfield Management Course
                                    HCITB trainer skills courses TS1, TS2,
                                    TS3, TS4
                                    Training development and analysis
                                    courses
Years in industry: 19

Job history

AGE	CAREER MOVES
16 years	General assistant - hotel
17 years	Nanny - USA (private house)
18½ years	Bar and kitchen work - pub/ restaurant
19½ years	Housekeeper/receptionist - hotel

AGE	CAREER MOVES	
20½ years	Junior assistant manager	) Multiple
	Assistant food and beverage	) hotel
	manager	) chain
	Assistant personnel manager	)
26½ years	Deputy manager	)
27½ years	Personnel manager - hotel	
28 years	Ran a recruitment agency in South Africa	
29 years	Training job - cosmetic firm	
31 years	Training Board - DMS qualification	
34 years	Present job	

Career outline

The respondent spent some time travelling abroad in the early
stages of her career doing a number of diffferent jobs. She
returned home in her early 20's when she took a job as a junior
assistant manager with a large hotel group where she stayed for six
years. During this time she developed skills in junior management

and in different areas of hotel work. Her reasons for leaving at this seemingly important stage in her career were because she had had enough of discrimination, with men in comparable positions to herself earning more and having better chances of promotion.

She then ran a recruitment agency in South Africa which gave the opportunity to travel. She left after a year: "I get bored quickly - I need scope and challenge, and I can generate the challenge for myself."

After spending some years with an Industrial Training Board the respondent joined her present company three years before the interview. She had had to develop the job into its present role and found this very rewarding. The role and function of the job currently needed reviewing.

The influences affecting choice of catering as a career

In her own words: "I hated school and its confines. I wanted to travel and to earn money. My family helped with my decision to go into catering, although I was vague about what to do at the beginning.

"Things just happened. I am not a career woman - I can't separate my job from life in general. I put the same energy into my job as I do into my life. I move from a job when I am bored, and when I stop learning."

Further career aspirations

The respondent expressed an interest in staying in her present company for 3-5 years more, although never wanted to remain static. She wished to pursue personnel and training related activities although she was inclined towards developing more creative and artistic skills. She felt however, that she would have to move outside her present company in order to achieve this.

CAREER HISTORY 6

Job and personal details

Job title: General catering manager
Level: Senior management
Type of establishment: Contract catering

Sex: Female
Age: 36 years
Marital status: Married
Qualifications: 7 'O'level equivalents
                              City and Guilds 150, 151, and
                              Waiting certificate (1965)
                              HCIMA (pilot scheme) (1969)
Training: HCITB instructor course
                              Supervision/management courses
                              3 day public speaking course
Years in industry: 20

Job history:

AGE	CAREER MOVES
16 years	College
18 years	Two year training scheme - hotels
20 years	Returned to college - HCIMA
21 years	General experience abroad for 3 years
24 years	Decimalisation trainer and member of a management relief team - industrial catering company
---------	--
25 years	Unit manager) promotion
	Area manager)
27 years	Residential unit manager
28 years	Set up main station bistro - British Rail
29 years	Production and selling - private gateaux company
29 years	Area manager - industrial catering
31-32 years	Regional operations manager - present company
35 years	General catering manager (present job)

Career outline

The respondent, after a relatively late start in comparison to other career histories, had acquired varied experiences, trying almost anything within the area of industrial/contract catering.

The influences affecting choice of catering as a career

The respondent could not identify any specific reasons for going into catering. When she left school (at 16 years of age) she felt she was not ready to go into the world of working. She described herself as 'a slow starter'.

"I don't really know why I went into the catering industry ... my parents felt that some sort of further education would be a stop gap ... there being very few options open where I lived - so I simply 'fell into' catering. I had no ambition to do anything at all - there was no pressure - I was just there."

Further career aspirations

The respondent said she was becoming increasingly interested in the commercial side of the business, that is in running a profit-making concern such as the one she was currently engaged in. Her previous experience had either been in subsidised catering, or commercial catering where making a profit had not been a priority.

Her present company intended to diversify and develop the commercial side of its activities. She therefore intended to "pitch herself up" to meet their requirements and make herself into "someone they can't overlook". She planned to develop with the company in what she saw as an exciting future.

CAREER HISTORY 7

Job and personal details

Job title: Director of sales and marketing
Level: Senior management
Type of establishment: Large city hotel

Sex: Female
Age: 36 years
Marital status: Single
Qualifications: 'O'levels
                              City and Guilds Advanced Dressmaking
                              and Design (1965)
                              Typing course (Pitmans) and basic
                              general office administration course
                              Institute of Sales and Marketing
                              (1968)
Training: Advanced marketing
                              Selling techniques
Years in industry   4

Job history

AGE	CAREER MOVES		
16 years	College		
17 years	Trainee fashion buyer - retail store		
19 years	A year off to pursue singing ambition		
20 years	Returned to college for shorthand course		
21 years	Secretary - accountancy firm		
27 years	Travel agent/sales executive		
	London sales executive	) car	
	Major accounts executive	) hire	
	European sales co-ordinator	) company	
32½ years	Sales executive		
---------	---		
34 years	Sales manager	)	
34½ years	Assistant director of sales	)present	
35½ years	Director of sales	)company	
	and marketing (present job)	)	

Career outline

The pattern of this career history is totally different from any
described previously. The respondent's initial qualifications
were in dressmaking and design and her initial training in fashion
buying. In fact she seemed to have had one or two 'false starts',
her career only really taking shape once she started working for a
car hire firm as a travel agent/sales executive.

Her first position with managerial responsibility came at the age of 34 when she joined her present company, her first venture into the hotel and catering industry, which she came into as a sales specialist rather than a caterer.

The respondent had achieved very senior management status in eight years after a very diverse career. She had set out with no aspirations at all and described herself as an opportunist.

The influences affecting choice of catering as a career

The respondent did not choose to work in the catering industry as such, but once involved found that she enjoyed it a great deal because of the variety, the people, the travel and the rewards of serving satisfied customers. "It is a tiring industry of which you never tire."

Further career aspirations

The respondent did not have any career aspirations or plans of any sort but was always "looking for new things". She did feel that she had found her niche in catering, not in terms of the catering aspect itself, but because it was a people industry. She described herself as a business woman, and she felt that she needed a job that would stimulate her mind.

Despite this lack of planning she did feel that in a year or two she would start thinking about what would be her next career move.

6 EXAMPLES OF MIXED STRATEGIES

Career histories 8 and 9 illustrate a mixed career strategy. There were critical points in the respondents' careers when a calculative strategy took over from an otherwise evolutionary career path.

Career history 8 is of a woman who started her career in house-keeping with a management level qualification. Although she had no career plans, when, at the age of 22, she found she liked her job in the personnel department of a large city hotel she made a definite decision to stay in this function and by the age of 25 she had become personnel manager.

Career history 9 is of a man with a management level qualification who had become group personnel manager for a hotel chain by the age of 28. His original objective was to make a career in line management (a calculative career strategy) but he drifted into an ancillary function (allowing his career to evolve).

CAREER HISTORY 8

Job and personal details

Job title: Personnel manager
Level: Senior management
Type of establishment: Large city hotel

Sex: Female
Age: 27 years
Marital status: Single
Qualifications: 8 'O' levels
                               3 'A' levels
                               HND Hotel and Catering Management (1977)
                               Institute of Personnel Management (1962)
Training: HCITB trainer skills courses TS1, TS2,
                               TS3
                               In-house training courses
Years in industry: 6½ (inclusive of industrial release
                               and part-time work)

Job history

AGE   CAREER MOVES
18 years   College - HND
20 years   Floor supervisor - hotel
21 years   Floor housekeeper   )
22½ years   Personnel assistant)   present
23½ years   Personnel officer   )   company
---------   --------------------)--------------------
25 years   Personnel manager   )

Career outline

The respondent started her career in housekeeping in hotels. After
a short time she decided to change because she felt there was no
control.

    Although she liked the hotel trade, she did not like the
catering operations side so she moved into personnel at the age of
21. She considered that she had found her niche.

The influences affecting choice of catering as a career

The respondent felt that she had not received good careers guidance
when she had to decide what she should do. The option of taking a
catering course was in effect an "insurance policy" against not
getting the appropriate grades to go to university.

    In fact she found the catering course enjoyable and felt it
provided her with good all-round knowledge. She said she "sailed
through it".

Further career aspirations

The respondent had no firm career plans. Having become involved in personnel she had enjoyed it and wished to develop within this sphere of activity.

She felt, however, that progress in personnel was very limited in hotels, unless she went to a larger hotel group. She thought that she had not enough experience yet for a move of this kind. She believed her career path would reveal itself and described herself as "relatively ambitious but not a back-stabber or I would have got further already".

She felt that the industry was geared to people knowing what they wanted to do, which was unfair in her opinion for two reasons. Firstly, she felt that many people came to the industry ill-prepared or poorly advised in terms of existing opportunities and secondly, some people might take longer than others to find their interest.

The respondent felt that one's career should be important as part of improving the quality of one's life, but should not be the first and only priority.

CAREER HISTORY 9

Job and personal details

Job title: Group personnel manager
Level: Senior management
Type of establishment: Large hotel within major hotel group

Sex: Male
Age: 37 years
Marital status: Married
Qualifications: 9 'O' levels
                              2 'A' levels
                              BSc Hotel & Catering Administration (1968)
                              MHCIMA (1969)
Training: All HCITB courses
                              Training officer's course
                              Sales and marketing
                              Industrial relations
                              Personnel skills
                              Decision making and problem solving
                              Appraisal skills
                              Interviewing and selection
                              Management principles
Years in industry   15

Job history

AGE	CAREER MOVES
22 years	Graduate trainee – brewery
23 years	Training officer – brewery
25 years	Group training officer – Training Board
————	————————————————————————————————
27 years	Personnel/training manager – hotel
28 years	Group personnel manager – hotel group (present job)

Career outline

The respondent joined a brewery company as a graduate trainee
immediately after leaving university. Shortly afterwards the
company merged with two other companies and the respondent had to
make a decision on whether to go into operational management or
into sales. He had the opportunity to develop some training skills
and so took the job of training officer, which subsequently led him
to work for the Training Board.

Having developed these training skills and contacts in the
industry, the respondent was offered a job as personnel and
training manager in a large hotel. From there he moved to his
present job which was an opportunity to get into what he described
as "a large expanding company".

Although his job had since then apparently remained the same, the respondent said that its function had changed in terms of scope and responsibility.

The influences affecting choice of catering as a career

The respondent decided when he was a teenager that he wanted to be a hotel manager. This decision followed a family holiday when he stayed in a hotel and became fascinated by the whole concept of hotels, and he felt that he would enjoy it.

He had a number of holiday jobs in hotels and decided he liked the industry. He enjoyed the variety, excitement, challenge, and unpredictability it offered and found it "a very nice way of doing business".

Further career aspirations

Although the respondent may be seen to have drifted into a 'staff role' rather than an operational role, with no apparent career plan, he certainly had a well thought-out future. In fact he described three alternatives from which he would eventually have to decide. At the time of the interview he wished to keep his options open for three to four years, then would have to make a decision. He was aware of opportunities other than those he had outlined and he was eager to keep an open mind, whilst at the same time developing himself for a particular goal.

7 WHAT ARE THE LESSONS TO BE LEARNT?

The foregoing career histories have shown that it is possible for both men and women to reach a high management level, whether they are following a calculative career strategy or an evolutionary one, or a mixture. Different personalities have followed different career philosophies. In principle one might expect those who pursue single-mindedly a calculative career strategy to obtain distinct advantages from so doing, in practise there are people who allow their career to evolve without planning and progress just as quickly.

However, for reasons explained in Part 1, the wisest course of action for anyone contemplating a career in hotel and catering management is to attempt some degree of planning in their career progression. The best method of becoming a 'high flyer' as the evidence of those interviewed shows, is to fit the structure of one's life and circumstances to long-term career aspirations, and to plan ahead. Whilst it is not always possible to timetable exactly the course of a career, regular reviews are a useful tactic, adopted in some measure by even the most 'evolutionary' of the 'high flyers'.

As the career histories also show, another important factor in successful career planning is to be aware of the limitations and restrictions to further advancements, and to be active in taking measures to correct them.

Career histories 10, 11 and 12 are of people who at the time of the interview were at a middle management level. They are presented as examples for those embarking on, or already involved in a career in hotel and catering management, who may wish to plot the possible next steps in the careers of these three people, and thereby help their own career planning.

CAREER HISTORY 10

Job and personal details

Job title: Assistant food and beverage manager
Level: Middle management
Type of establishment: Large hotel within a major group

Sex: Male
Age: 23 years
Marital status: Single (engaged to be married)
Qualifications: 5 'O' levels
                      OND Hotel and Catering Operations (1978)
                      HCIMA Part B (1980)
Training: Management principles
                      Employee relations
                      Interview/selection
                      Appraisal
Years in industry: 10 (including vacation work and
                      industrial release while at college)

Job history

AGE	CAREER MOVES
13-16 years	Part-time work during weekends and school holidays
16 years	College OND
18 years	HCIMA Part B including 2 x 3 months industrial release periods
20 years	Joined present company as a trainee Reception shift leader) Chief steward) Training Banqueting supervisor) programme Food & beverage cost control)
21½ years	Assistant food and beverage manager (present job)

Career outline

The respondent had been involved in some aspect of restaurant or hotel work since 13 years of age, accumulating many years experience considering his young age.

  After obtaining his HCIMA Part B qualification he immediately joined his present company, where he became a company trainee and carried out a training programme.

  His present job of assistant food and beverage manager is likely to be the starting point of his future career.

The influences affecting a choice of catering as a career

The respondent had family connections in catering - his grand-
parents owned a hotel with which he was involved from an early age,
and his uncle had a public house.

During his teens he was impressed by the achievement of one of
his friends who worked in a restaurant some evenings and weekends
and earned a good deal more than the respondent who was doing a
paper-round: "I was earning 90p per week getting up at 5.30 am in
all weathers and he was getting £4.50 per week in much nicer
conditions."

He therefore found a job as a waiter at the age of 13. He
was however tall enough to pass as 15. He enjoyed this work
enormously, and made contact with students from the local college
who gave him information about the OND course that he eventually
took.

Further career aspirations

The respondent outlined four career options facing him, about which
he would make a decision fairly quickly. Firstly he could remain
with his present company and given that he would continue at his
present rate of progress, in under ten years he was likely to be a
general manager. This option would ensure a certain degree of
security.

His second option attracted him most: to start up his own
business. It would entail going abroad where, in his view, he
would have more chance of raising the capital needed.

He felt that if he was going to follow this option he should
have to do so quickly, so that if he failed he would still be young
enough to resume his career.

The respondent's third option was to move to a five star
operation. His fourth was to leave the hotel sector and go into
industrial catering for a job with less hours and more pay (he was
not strongly attracted to this idea).

CAREER HISTORY 11

Job and personal details

Job title: Unit catering manager
Level: Middle management
Type of establishment: Contract catering outlet belonging
                              major group

Sex: Female
Age: 22 years
Marital status: Single
Qualifications: 3 CSE
                              1 'O' level
                              OND Hotel and Catering Operations (1980)
Training: Induction   )
                              Basic food preparation)
                              Accounts   ) Part of
                              Health & safety   ) management
                              Interviewing   ) training
                              Marketing   ) scheme
                              Purchasing   )
                              HCITB TS1   )
Years in industry: 3

Job history

AGE   CAREER MOVES
17 years   College (OND)
19 years   Assistant cook   ) Present
20 years   Management trainee   ) company
--------   ----------------------)---------------
20½ years   Assistant manager   )
22 years   Unit catering manager   )
                              (present job)

Career outline

The respondent joined her present employer straight from college
and took up the position of assistant cook, which she held for a
year. Although not the initial intention she was then recruited on
to the company's management training programme. This included head
office courses and on-the-job training and her experience as
assistant cook was counted as part of her programme.
    She was then moved to another unit as an assistant manager,
and three weeks before the interview had been promoted to unit
catering manager.

The influences affecting choice of catering as a career

The respondent said that she had enjoyed cookery at school and had enquired about opportunities in catering. She was accepted at college, and chose the OND because she wanted something "with a bit more management in it". She wanted to keep her options open rather than concentrate on a craft course.

Her original intention was to go into hotels, but not only did she have difficulty getting a job, but she was told that as a woman she would have great difficulty getting into management in hotels.

This prompted her to go into industrial catering, and she was very pleased to have made this decision because hotel work would be "so disruptive to my life".

Further career aspirations

The respondent had ambitions to reach the level of area catering supervisor, and ultimately area manager. She had not given this a great deal of thought however, since she had only just begun her present job, and wanted to "take things one at a time".

She said that she liked training and might try to attach herself to the training department. She had no definite plans however for any particular course of action.

CAREER HISTORY 12

Job and personal details

Job title: Area manager
Level: Middle management
Type of establishment: Large contract catering firm

Sex: Female
Age: 27 years old
Marital status: Married
Qualifications: 8 'O' levels
                      OND Hotel and Catering Operations (1974)
Training: Basic management course
                      Personnel
                      HCITB trainer skills course TS1
                      Target setting
                      Appraisal interviewing
                      Trade union negotiation
                      RIPHH
                      HCITB/Cranfield - management
Years in industry   8

Job history

AGE	CAREER MOVES
16 years	College (OND)
18 years	1 year sandwich course HCIMA (failed)
19 years	Junior assistant manager) Atomic
	) Energy
20 years	Assistant manager) Authority
22 years	Worked for six weeks with her husband as an assistant management couple in a hotel
22 years	Husband and wife management team - golf club
23 years	Returned home to family business helping out - garden centre
23½ years	Assistant unit manager) present
24½ years	Unit manager) company
25½ years	Area manager (present job))

Career outline

The respondent had a very rapid start to her career, getting a
position as a junior assistant manager with the Atomic Energy
Authority. In this position she was responsible for the catering
requirements of scientific visitors, and for the domestic
arrangements in the hostel. She was quickly promoted to assistant
manager, a position she held for two years until she left to get
married.

She and her husband joined a scheme as an assistant management couple in a hotel in order to gain some formal management experience and training, but left after six weeks, unhappy with the methods of the hotel manager and the hotel environment.

They then worked as a husband and wife team for a year, running a golf club. They left this position because they decided that they were 'not getting very far'. They both wished to rethink their careers so returned home to work in the family business and give themselves time to decide on their future.

They then returned to London and both obtained jobs with different branches of the respondent's present company.

The respondent described herself as having done a number of different and varied things early on in her career, getting a wide range of both craft and management experience.

The influences affecting choice of catering as a career

The respondent did not know what to do when she left school, she was only interested in leaving. But her uncle was a chef, so she decided to do catering. She originally wanted to do a reception course but she was told that she was over-qualified for this so she did an OND.

Further career aspirations

The respondent had no plans in terms of timescales and strategies but she did have very definite ideas about the management level she wished to reach.

It was only after being in the industry for a short time, and having the opportunity to compare herself to others, that she decided she could do a better job of management, even with her little experience. She became ambitious for the first time.

She wanted to get on to regional management level and from there go into a different aspect of catering. She felt that she had been in contract catering for too long; the growth years of her career had all been with one company, in one region and only dealing with one aspect of it. Although she recognised that she was in a very commercial environment in her present company and this was true of contract catering generally, she felt that the working atmosphere was still welfare-oriented.

She wanted to obtain a regional management level job, so that via this position she would accumulate enough confidence in her own style and ability to be able to assess herself and use her skills elsewhere. From there she would look for a general management position. She felt that it was important for her to "expand her base", make herself "worth something to other parts of the industry" and have "a career history that shows versatility". She felt that she would achieve this by pushing for the things she wanted as the opportunities arose.

The respondent also felt that it was important to have reached a senior corporate level position before leaving to have children. Her opinion was that having reached this level her broad management skills would have been developed so that the break to have children would not be too disruptive to her career.

PART 3

QUESTIONNAIRE

```
                                        |___|___|___|___|___|
                                        HCITB  Sec  Serial Number
                                        REGION tor
```

WOMEN IN MANAGEMENT QUESTIONNAIRE

1a. Job Title .... |___|___|

1b. Group .... |___|___|

2.   Sex | Male | 1 |
                  | Female | 2 |

3.   Age |___|___|

4.   Marital Status

     | Single | 1 |
     | Married | 2 |
     | Separated | 3 |
     | Divorced | 4 |
     | Widow | 5 |

5.   Do you have children or other dependants?   YES |_1_| NO |_2_|
                                                                     GO TO 6a

     a) If YES age of children   Age |___|
                                             |___|
                                             |___|
                                             |___|
                                             |___|

     b) Details of other dependants ....

         ....

         ....

6a. Spouses/partners occupation .... |___|___|

6b. How long has your husband/wife/partner been in his/her
     present job?................................ |___|___|

7. Please tell me the job title of your direct superior.

Job Title .... | | | |

Sex .... | M | 1 |
                      | F | 2 |

8. Please tell me the job title of your direct subordinate.

		M	F	JOB TITLE CODE	
Job Title		1	2		
Job Title		1	2		
Job Title		1	2		
Job Title		1	2		

9. Listed below are various attributes and skills which could be necessary for managers in the Hotel & Catering Industry to have in order to carry out their jobs.

Please could you rank them twice - first indicating how necessary you think they are to any manager in the Hotel and Catering Industry and then how confident you feel in your own ability to carry them out.

Show: Scale/cards

		UN	FN	VN	AE	VU	FU	C	VC
1.	Being well organised & methodical	1	2	3	4	1	2	3	4
2.	Having knowledge of safety & hygiene	1	2	3	4	1	2	3	4
3.	Able to work in extremes of heat	1	2	3	4	1	2	3	4
4.	Thinking ahead	1	2	3	4	1	2	3	4
5.	Working under a lot of pressure	1	2	3	4	1	2	3	4
6.	Knowing rules of the organisation	1	2	3	4	1	2	3	4
7.	Knowing the law relating to your job	1	2	3	4	1	2	3	4
8.	Being able to work very quickly	1	2	3	4	1	2	3	4
9.	Having physical strength	1	2	3	4	1	2	3	4
10.	Having the ability to communicate (verbally) with customers	1	2	3	4	1	2	3	4
11.	Communicating well with other employees	1	2	3	4	1	2	3	4
12.	Giving clear written instructions	1	2	3	4	1	2	3	4
13.	Understanding written instructions	1	2	3	4	1	2	3	4
14.	Being able to use the telephone well	1	2	3	4	1	2	3	4
15.	Working knowledge of a foreign language	1	2	3	4	1	2	3	4
16.	Giving clear instructions	1	2	3	4	1	2	3	4
17.	Understanding how customers think	1	2	3	4	1	2	3	4
18.	Having a pleasant manner	1	2	3	4	1	2	3	4
19.	Looking smart/tidy	1	2	3	4	1	2	3	4
20.	Being a good member of a team	1	2	3	4	1	2	3	4
21.	Having a good memory	1	2	3	4	1	2	3	4
22.	Having artistic flair/imagination	1	2	3	4	1	2	3	4
23.	Having knowledge of basic maths	1	2	3	4	1	2	3	4
24.	Meeting deadlines	1	2	3	4	1	2	3	4
25.	Being alert	1	2	3	4	1	2	3	4
26.	Dealing with emergencies	1	2	3	4	1	2	3	4
27.	Dealing with complaints	1	2	3	4	1	2	3	4
28.	Having a clear speaking voice	1	2	3	4	1	2	3	4
29.	Being prepared to turn your hand to anything	1	2	3	4	1	2	3	4
30.	Using your own initiative	1	2	3	4	1	2	3	4

		U N	F N	V N	A E	V U	F U	C	V C
31.	Being a leader	1	2	3	4	1	2	3	4
32.	Having a knowledge of fire procedures	1	2	3	4	1	2	3	4
33.	Knowling the layout of the establishment	1	2	3	4	1	2	3	4
34.	Being discreet	1	2	3	4	1	2	3	4
35.	Being observant	1	2	3	4	1	2	3	4
36.	Being reliable/responsible	1	2	3	4	1	2	3	4
37.	Being patient	1	2	3	4	1	2	3	4
38.	Being honest	1	2	3	4	1	2	3	4
39.	Working well with your hands	1	2	3	4	1	2	3	4
40.	Being self disciplined	1	2	3	4	1	2	3	4
41.	Being punctual	1	2	3	4	1	2	3	4
42.	Being in good health	1	2	3	4	1	2	3	4
43.	Having a sense of humour	1	2	3	4	1	2	3	4
44.	Being accurate	1	2	3	4	1	2	3	4
45.	Being self-controlled	1	2	3	4	1	2	3	4
46.	Having stamina	1	2	3	4	1	2	3	4
47.	Being a good salesman	1	2	3	4	1	2	3	4

10. How long have you worked for this company? |___|___|
                                                      YEARS

11. Is this your only job since joining the Company?   YES |_1_| NO |_2_|
                                                        IF YES GO   IF NO GO
                                                          TO 13   TO 12

12. If NO what jobs and how long did you hold them?

POSITION	CODE	DEPARTMENT	CODE	TIME SPENT	REASON FOR CHANGE

- 3 -

13. How long have you worked in the Hotel & Catering Industry?

YEARS

14. Please give me details of your Job History in chronological order (from school, college etc. also include any time off for child-rearing etc.)

Job Title	Sector	Length of Stay	Reason for leaving	Main Responsibility

15. Do you have any qualifications or training?   YES | 1 | NO | 2 |

GO TO 15

If YES: please tell me all of them: (school, college, professional, include training).

16a. SCHOOL

Type	Code	Date

- 4 -

16b. COLLEGE/PROFESSIONAL

Qualifications	Code	Date

16c. TRAINING (not college)

Type	Code	Date	In-company	External

17a. What are your career aspirations over the next 10 years. Would you like to:

		YES	NO
a.	stay where you are	☐	☐
b.	change your job but do similar work	☐	☐
c.	change your career entirely	☐	☐
d.	progress further in your present job (without promotion)	☐	☐
e.	reach a more senior level by obtaining promotion	☐	☐
f.	get to the top of your profession	☐	☐
g.	take time off for child rearing but return to work later	☐	☐
h.	other (please specify)		

17b. Please tell me why you wish to follow this career path ....

....

....

....

....

....

....

....

....

....

....

....

....

....

....

....

....

17c. and how you hope to achieve it ....

....

....

18. Are you given information of your company's training policy?

YES | 1 | NO | 2 |

if YES please give details ....

....

....

19a. Do you think you would benefit from any of the following
training?

                                                          YES   NO

- Basic technical or skills training | | | |

- Advance technical or skills training | | | |

- Councelling on career developments | | | |

- Communications/organised training | | | |

- Training for a professional qualification | | | |

- Management training | | | |

- No further training | | | |

- Other (please specify) ....

....

19b. Why do you think you need this? ....

....

....

....

....

....

....

....

19c. How do you think you will achieve it? ....

....

....

....

....

....

....

....

....

....

....

....

....

20. What assistance/encouragement do you think you will receive from your
company?

....

....

....

....

....

....

....

....

....

....

....

....

21. The following items are an attempt to assess the attitudes people have about women in business. The best answer to each statement is your honest personal opinion. The statements cover many different and opposing points of view; you may find yourself agreeing strongly with some statements, disagreeing just as strongly with others and perhaps uncertain about others. Whether you agree or disagree with any statements you can be sure that many people feel the same as you.

(Interviewer: Give scale cards/show card)

Please look at the scale card and tell me the number that indicates your rating.

	SD	D	SD	NDA	SA	A	SA
1. It is less desirable for women than for men to have a job that requires responsibility.	1	2	3	4	5	6	7
2. Women have the objectivity required to evaluate business situations properly.	1	2	3	4	5	6	7
3. Challenging work is more important to men than it is to women.	1	2	3	4	5	6	7
4. Men and women should be given equal opportunity for participants in management training programs.	1	2	3	4	5	6	7
5. Women have the capability to acquire the necessary skills to be successful managers.	1	2	3	4	5	6	7
6. On the average, women managers are less capable of contributing to an organization's overall goals than are men.	1	2	3	4	5	6	7
7. It is not acceptable for women to assume leadership roles as often as men.	1	2	3	4	5	6	7
8. The business community should someday accept women in key managerial positions.	1	2	3	4	5	6	7
9. Society should regard work by female managers as valuable as work by male managers.	1	2	3	4	5	6	7
10. It is acceptable for women to compete with men for top executive positions.	1	2	3	4	5	6	7
11. The possibility of pregnancy does not make women less desirable employees than men.	1	2	3	4	5	6	7
12. Women would no more allow their emotions to influence their managerial behaviour than would men.	1	2	3	4	5	6	7
13. Problems associated with menstruation should not make women less desirable than men as employees.	1	2	3	4	5	6	7
14. To be a successful executive, a women does not have to sacrifice some of her femininity.	1	2	3	4	5	6	7
15. On the average, a women who stays at home all the time with her children is a better mother than a women who works outside the home at least half the time.	1	2	3	4	5	6	7

	SD	D	SD	NDA	SA	A	SA
16. Women are less capable of learning mathematical and mechanical skills than are men.	1	2	3	4	5	6	7
17. Women are not ambitious enough to be successful in the business world.	1	2	3	4	5	6	7
18. Women cannot be assertive in business situations that demand it.	1	2	3	4	5	6	7
19. Women possess the self-confidence required of a good leader.	1	2	3	4	5	6	7
20. Women are not competitive enough to be successful in the business world.	1	2	3	4	5	6	7
21. Women cannot be aggressive in business situations that demand it.	1	2	3	4	5	6	7

(One page was allowed on the original questionnaire to each of the following questions.)

22. Please tell me about the influences which helped you decide on a career in catering. (Probe)

23. Are there any personal/financial committment which you need to consider before making career decision (e.g. family, mortgage, friends).

24. What opportunities do you think there are for women within the catering industry. (Probe hours, lifestyle, training, attitudes etc.)

25. Given the high % of women within the catering industry and the relatively few who reach supervisory/management levels. What in your opinion are the problems women encounter on their path to the management jobs. (e.g. mens attitudes, womens attitudes, problems of assertion, family, publics image of catering industry).